Nature's Sc

Margaret Fetty

Contents

Rigby

A Harcourt Achieve Imprint

www.Rigby.com
1-800-531-5015

Water, Wind, and Ice

Dark clouds race high overhead.
A gust of wind swirls sand and dirt
into the air.
Before long, rain bursts from the sky.
Water races across the ground and
cuts tiny streams into the soil.

The storm is over quickly, but the
blowing wind and flowing water
have changed the earth's surface.

The earth is always changing.
Water, wind, and ice are **forces**
that have the power to shape the land.
They move against the earth and
cause small pieces of sand, rocks, and
dirt to break off.
This movement is called **erosion**.

rocks broken by erosion

In a heavy rainstorm, erosion can
change the land quickly.
The wind moves sand and dirt,
and the water cuts small paths
in the ground.

Water, wind, and ice can also work
for millions of years to create
beautiful giant sculptures, or shapes,
on the land.
Erosion can create arches, **monuments**,
canyons, and other interesting shapes.

one of nature's sculptures

Rock Arches

At one time, the land in Arches National Park in Utah was one giant rock with long cracks on the surface.

Over a very long time, water and ice in the cracks made the cracks grow larger.

Then the rocks split into long blocks. Sand and rocks, carried by the wind and water, made holes, or small arches, in the blocks.
Rainwater moved over the blocks, too, and made the holes larger.
These forces have created over 2,000 arches in this park.

a large arch made by wind and water

How Arches Are Formed

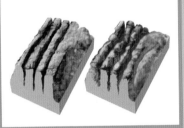

large cracks made by water and ice

more space between cracks made by water and ice

small arch made by wind and water

View a Hoodoo

Visitors to Bryce Canyon in Utah like to see the hoodoos. Hoodoos are rocks that have interesting shapes.

Some hoodoos are tall and pointed, while others are short and round. Some of these rocks even look like castles or animals.

hoodoos in Bryce Canyon

Monuments Up High

In Utah's Monument Valley, many
rock towers rise high into the air.
At one time, this land was high
and level.
It was called a plateau, and it looked
flat like the top of a table.

Water cut the plateau into parts.
Sand blowing in the wind cut more
of the plateau away.
That left behind beautiful, tall
monuments that show how nature's
forces work.

a monument in
Monument Valley

A Grand Canyon

The Grand Canyon in Arizona is the best known of nature's sculptures. The Colorado River has flowed through this canyon for millions of years.

The forces of the river and erosion have made the Grand Canyon more than one mile deep and 15 miles wide in places.

The Grand Canyon is changing slowly. The flow of the Colorado River, along with wind and ice erosion, continue to shape it.

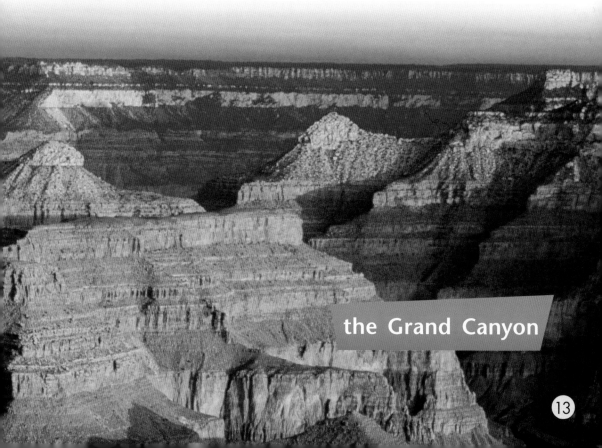

the Grand Canyon

The Changing Earth

Erosion will change all of
nature's sculptures over time.
The arches, hoodoos, and monuments
will slowly erode away.
The smaller pieces will be moved
to new places, while the bigger pieces
will stay on the ground.

Erosion will continue to build and shape the land in other places. There will always be new sculptures to enjoy.

Glossary

erosion the wearing away of the earth's surface by water, wind, or ice

forces things that can move, stop, or change the direction of other objects

monuments places of great natural beauty set aside by a government

Index